BURNED OUT!

A TEACHER SPEAKS OUT
by Jack Dewey

Illustrated by Jeff Danziger

The New England Press
Shelburne, Vermont

© 1986 by The New England Press, Inc.
All Rights Reserved
ISBN 0-933050-37-2
Library of Congress Catalog Card Number: 86-60763
Printed in the United States of America
Second Printing, March 1989

For additional copies of this book or for a copy of our catalog, please write:

The New England Press
P.O. Box 575
Shelburne, VT 05482

*This book is dedicated to all teachers
who take themselves too seriously.*

Contents

Introduction

My name is Jack Dewey and I'm a burnt-out teacher. Or should I just say a worn-out teacher? Until I left teaching in 1984, I was feeling a bit like Edna St. Vincent Millay who burned her candle at both ends. My wick just wasn't what it used to be. During my sixteen years as a history teacher, I must have taught the causes of the Civil War a hundred times and at least ten different ways. It got so that I could walk into a classroom and switch on the automatic lecture pilot. Sometimes I would wake up in the middle of a sentence and wonder how to get out of it. Other times my mind would float to the back of the classroom to watch the body teach and say, "Oh no, Jack, not another discussion on Andrew Jackson and the Rise of the Common Man!" In short, it was time to take a long break from the classroom.

Still, even during the last few years, the old flame would return on occasion. It usually happened when the conversation drifted for one reason or another to cross-country bike trips, Vietnam, or why there were no blacks in our school. Then the old liberal juices would start flowing again, and I

would curse the ding-dong who invented the passing bell. When the class was a dud, however, that was the time they would work on the school's clocks and my class would run over by ten minutes.

I'm no longer a practicing teacher. But while it's easy enough to take the teacher out of the school, it's much harder to take the school out of the teacher. I've spent many hours thinking about schools and about teaching. I know now that I'll always have a love/hate relationship with public education. That ambivalence has made this a difficult book to write. Sometimes I miss my old role so much that I'll launch into a lecture on Benvenuto Cellini whenever someone mentions the Renaissance or spinach lasagna. Other times I wonder how I ever survived sixteen years in the classroom.

Be that as it may, you don't spend sixteen years as a schoolteacher without coming away with a thought or two. The purpose of this book is to let off some steam and to give you the benefit of my experience. It tells my views on what students, teachers, administrators, and parents are really like. It defines the "good" teacher and the "bad" teacher, it tests the most basic assumptions about education, and it offers a clearcut proposal for reforming the schools. It also provides a straightforward, no-nonsense dictionary guide through the thicket of educational jargon. In short, this book is the kind of personal assessment of the public schools that you'll never find in any of those overblown "major commission studies" that have been done on public schools in recent years.

1 *Why Some People Love to Hate Teachers*

Most people aren't neutral about teachers the way they might be neutral about, say, bank tellers or hardware-store owners. Each of us has known a teacher we didn't like. Each of us has had a teacher who made us stand in the corner or assigned too much homework or rapped our knuckles. In any event, there is abroad in the land a distrust for most teachers. Here are some of the common reasons why teachers are generally held in such low esteem and why they get kicked around so much by the public.

The teacher is handy. As a local government employee, he or she is the one person on the public payroll whose throat the people can get their hands around. The state and federal governments are beyond reach. What can the people really do about a scandal in Albany or Boston or Sacramento? And what can the people really do to the Defense Department if it squanders billions of dollars on a missile that never flies off the drawing board? In most cases, not much. But if the local teachers ask for something, watch out! That's one tax dollar they're not going to get!

Teachers are aiding and abetting the spread of the new illiteracy. SAT scores fell for nearly two decades, so it must be the teachers' fault. Curriculum changes in the late 1960's and the early 1970's that emphasized "value clarification" and "relevancy" at the expense of the basics are partly to blame. But the significance of television and two working parents in undermining reading and writing skills is hard to overestimate. But, what the hell, it's more fun to nail the teachers.

Taxpayers think teachers are overpaid. Teachers work only half the year and get a full year's salary. Some old fossils on maximum salary, who are just going through the motions, *are* overpaid! But look at a first-year teacher who has four or five preparations a night and pulls down a salary of $13,000. That's candy-striper pay.

The public resents tenure. Most jobs don't come with a lifetime guarantee. A good point. In most school systems, a teacher has to become a flaming nitwit, an outrageous embarrassment, or a sex pervert before there is even the possibility that he or she might get fired.

Teachers aren't very smart. People who majored in education in college were ranked socially by the rest of the student population below everyone including art and business majors. How many times have you heard the expression, "Those who can, do; those who can't, teach; and those who can't teach, teach teachers?"

People don't like the way teachers spend their days. The way the average citizen sees the teacher's day goes something like this: 7:00-7:30 A.M.: drive to school; 7:30-2:30: teach four or five classes, relax in the teachers' lounge, and play hard-to-find; 2:30-5:30: nine quick holes of golf or an extended happy hour at a nearby watering hole; 5:30-7:00: a leisurely dinner with imported wine; 7:00-11:00: watch TV or take in an evening at the dog track; 11:00: go to bed.

Teachers, of course, see the same day in a totally different way: 7:00–7:30 A.M.: drive to school; 7:30–2:30: teach six classes, patrol the corridors, answer the phone, dodge insults, eat lunch in ten minutes; 2:30–3:30: meet with students and parents; 3:30–4:00: drive home; 4:00–4:05: play with your own children; 4:05–6:00: grade papers and call parents; 6:00–6:10: eat a TV dinner; 6:10–9:00: attend a graduate course at Upper Creek State College; 9:00–midnight: grade more papers and prepare for the next day's classes; midnight–1:00 A.M.: read *NEA Today*; 1:00–2:30 A.M.: do reading and research assigned from the graduate course at Upper Creek State College; 2:30–6:30 A.M.: insomnia.

Teachers whine and "cry wolf" too much. Tax-cutting measures like Proposition 13 in California and Proposition 2½ in Massachusetts were going to destroy "the foundations of education as we have known it," according to the teacher unions. The same arguments were used against Reagan's election and his reelection. Despite teacher protests, the sky didn't fall even once.

Who cares about teachers anyway? Twenty years ago, one out of every two taxpayers had a direct interest in the local school system because their kids were in it. Today, less than one out of four taxpayers has children attending public schools.

2 *Classroom Styles*

I became a teacher almost by accident. Teaching certainly wasn't one of my childhood dreams, which were crowded with visions of hitting .400, breaking the sound barrier, and starring in the movies. Still, in 1967, I needed a job—any job. The promise of short hours and long vacations made teaching seem attractive. And, since I was single at the time and could easily survive on Cheerios, popcorn, and beer, the $5,200 salary wasn't much of a deterrent. So I applied for a social studies position in Billerica, Massachusetts. I got the job mainly because I was 6'3", had been to Vietnam, and read *Time* magazine.

Somehow, one thing led to another and sixteen years later I woke up and found out that I was still a teacher. During that time I was everything from a very good teacher to a rather mediocre teacher. Some teachers seem to be immortal. They start out as great teachers and just keep on going. Not me. I belonged to the more organic variety of teacher who goes through the cycle of birth, growth, decay, and death.

I started out on the weak side. During my first year at

Billerica my major strength was my ability to break up fights. I once broke up a scuffle between two junior high school boys. I put each kid in a headlock and, with heels dragging, carted them off to the vice principal's office where I dropped them on the floor. That display impressed the hell out of the kids ("Wow, that's Mr. Dewey. Hasn't he been to Vietnam?") and astonished my fellow teachers.

In the meantime, I was picking up my master's degree at Salem State College and learning that mugging students (even in the line of duty) wasn't approved pedagogy. So I began to mellow. I took to flowered ties, yellow glasses, long sideburns and a "please-call-me-Jack" approach to teaching. That, of course, got me fired in June. Well, I wasn't exactly fired. School principals rarely have the guts for such clean-cut solutions. I was brought in for a conference the last day of the school year and told that some members of the community—not the principal himself, mind you—objected to my appearance. If I didn't change my attitude immediately, I was told, the principal would ride my case all the next year. At this point, I took the course of least resistance and told him to take the job and shove it.

After a year in a doctoral program at the University of Massachusetts, I moved on to teach in a small high school in Vermont. It was there, I think, that I hit my stride as a teacher. I felt good about what I was doing. I taught all the social studies classes to all levels of students. I coached softball and basketball. I organized student fasts for OXFAM. Students were welcome to come to my home at any time—and they did. I took a group of students to stay with Gov. John Gilligan at the executive mansion in Columbus, Ohio. (Gilligan was running for reelection and his son, Donald, invited me to bring some students to Columbus to view the election. Unfortunately, Gilligan was the only major incumbent Democrat to be defeated in the Watergate elections of 1974). I even took

hauling two kids to the office

a couple of students to Central America for two weeks on a totally unstructured tour. We flew to Gautemala and had to make our way, somehow, to Costa Rica by way of El Salvador.

After six years in Vermont I moved back to Massachusetts where the salaries were better. And a new school brought new challenges. I coached baseball for three years and developed a European history program where none had existed before. Then, slowly, I began to feel the numbness set in. I found myself assigning fewer papers and showing more filmstrips. I stopped coaching, and because I lived too far away, no kids dropped by the house. I knew I was in deep trouble when I started to count the days until June. Just the thought of another September was enough to make me want to retch. I was becoming another burnt-out teacher. So, after eight years of slow but steady incineration, I decided it was time to look elsewhere for something to do.

As I look back on those sixteen years of teaching, I don't see one seamless thread. It's more like a series of ink blots. I see that I've been not one teacher but several different kinds of teacher—some good, some not so good.

If you've ever been a teacher or a student, you'll recognize the following basic types of teacher.

MR. (MS.) CHIPS

The born teacher. In any century, in any town, in any pay scale, Mr. Chips would be a teacher. Mr. Chips is the type who would volunteer for duty at the Alamo so he could teach an adult education class in needlepoint—he'd teach anything anywhere. Every school needs its Mr. or Ms. Chips. This teacher will always do a great job regardless of whether he or she is appreciated or not. And he or she couldn't care less about changing fashions in teaching. Mr. Chips never left the basics.

Mr. Chips does, however, come in different flavors. There's the all-around Mr. Chips who knows his subject inside out, teaches all levels of students, opens his house to students, and coaches a couple of sports. I've known hundreds of teachers but only two who qualify for the all-around Mr. Chips label.

Then there is the limited-edition Mr. Chips. This version is also a great teacher, but only if he gets the bright classes. This Mr. Chips can't handle the slow learners or the juvenile delinquent types. When the limited-edition Mr. Chips becomes the department head, he picks all the honors classes for himself.

Mr. Chips

THE COACH

The Coach is a real athletic supporter. He is to the sports teams what Mr. Chips is to the classroom. The Coach usually teaches social studies or gym because they're the easiest subject areas in which to get certified. The Coach can always be found in the teachers' lounge diagramming off-tackle plays on a napkin or writing up a practice schedule in his planbook. For some strange reason, the Coach never seems to have any papers to grade. Maybe the Touchdown Club grades his papers. In the classroom, the Coach teaches by the numbers and tries to stay at least one chapter ahead of the kids. The Coach is a coach first, last, and always. Teaching is viewed as a necessary evil.

THE BLUE COLLAR

Perhaps the single largest group of teachers. The Blue Collar is perfectly happy to be a teacher and perfectly competent. The Blue Collar doesn't have the intellectual credentials of Mr. and Ms. Chips, but he has already forgotten more subject matter than the Coach ever knew. The Blue Collar will chaperon dances, serve on curriculum committees, and support the athletic teams. The Blue Collar likes the security that goes with tenure. Once the Blue Collar finds a school he likes, he stays there until they measure him for a pine box.

THE ROOKIE

Any teacher with less than three years' experience. The Rookie is a welcomed breath of fresh air to any school. She will often challenge the assumptions of her older colleagues.

The Rookie is always surrounded by kids because they appreciate her enthusiasm. The Rookie thinks a seventy-hour work week is normal. The Rookie will also volunteer to coach any sport where a coach is needed. Of all the teacher types, the Rookie is the poorest paid and the last one to complain. The Rookie is also a lock to get the largest classes and the worst kids. That's because the department head and the older teachers get the pick of the litter. As one of my former department heads loved to say, "Rank has its privileges."

THE MAGICIAN

The Magician is famous for his disappearing act. He's there at his desk at 2:45. But at 2:50 the Magician is long gone and hard to find. On cold winter days, he will sneak out of the school a few minutes early just to warm up his car. The Magician always volunteers to serve on *two* committees. That way he can always say he was attending the *other* committee meeting. Famed for his true/false tests, the Magician's briefcase is strictly for appearance only.

THE SILVER SCREEN

This teacher got her master's degree from the Sack Cinema. Mushrooms grow in her room because she never pulls up the shades. The Silver Screen's idea of developing a lesson plan is to read *TV Guide*. She then videotapes anything and everything that is remotely relevant to the curriculum. She shows the tapes to all her classes the next day on the school's VCR for which she has signed up weeks in advance. There's nothing like a seven-hour docudrama on George Washington or Christopher Columbus to kill a few classes. Even the students of the Silver Screen complain, "Do we have to see another film today?"

THE CINDER

And, finally, there is the Cinder, a.k.a. the Burnout. The Cinder regards handing out bookslips, grading plagiarized essays, and taking attendance as the intellectual equivalent of buying diapers, mowing the lawn, and changing the sheets. Every year the kids change, but the Cinder just gets older and older. The Cinder needs to find another job, but first he must find the courage to look.

the Cinder

3 Good Teachers and Bad Teachers

Getting out of the classroom can put things in perspective. At least it can put things in the perspective of a burnt-out teacher who has been both a good teacher and a bad teacher. So, after nearly two decades in the educational business, here are my working definitions of the "good" teacher and the "bad" teacher.

Good teachers call in sick on a Tuesday or a Wednesday. Bad teachers call in sick on a Monday or a Friday.

Both good teachers and bad teachers have "teacher" nightmares. In the good teacher's dream, he gets halfway through his lecture only to discover that he's not wearing any pants. In the bad teacher's dream, the students are the ones who are naked from the waist down.

Good teachers don't refer to the outside world as the "real world." They know that being a public-school teacher is real enough.

Good teachers don't raise their voices simply because they don't know what they are talking about.

Good teachers do not fear the competency test for themselves or for their students. Bad teachers fear both.

Good teachers stand their ground during a food fight in the cafeteria. Bad teachers go running off to find the vice principal or stick their heads out the faculty room door to laugh at those colleagues caught in the food fight.

Bad teachers don't know the difference between schooling and education. Good teachers know the limits of the classroom and don't ask themselves or their kids to do the impossible.

Good teachers know that a family trip to the West Indies just might be more educational than another week in their class. So the good teacher signs the permission slip.

Good teachers are still teaching when the bell rings even if only a couple of kids are still listening. Most kids have sat through enough fifty-minute classes so that they don't even have to look at the clock to know when there are just two minutes left. These kids take this time to plan how best to use the five-minute break between periods.

Bad teachers dread the coming of September, parents' night, report cards, and notes to see the principal. Good teachers dread only the note from the principal. They look forward to September, can defend their system of evaluation, and love to outline their programs to parents.

Good teachers aren't afraid to admit that there are some kids they just can't handle.

Good teachers are willing to share the burden of teaching the lower-level classes with other members of the department. While some teachers *want* to teach slower kids, most don't. The emotional drain is much greater and so is the burnout factor. Have you ever noticed how many ads there are in the newspaper for special-needs teachers, especially halfway through the school year?

Good teachers have done something else with their lives besides teach. Bad teachers get all bent out of shape when this is mentioned to them.

16

Good teachers know that a good faculty begins with a good English teacher. Bad teachers are interested only in protecting their own department's turf.

Bad English and social studies teachers get really riled at the mere suggestion that special bonuses be offered to attract more competent math and science majors into teaching.

Good teachers talk to people who are not teachers once in a while. Bad teachers don't know people who are not teachers.

Good teachers don't ask the students to call them by their first names.

Bad teachers love automatic pay increases, tenure, the Xerox machine, and textbooks with detailed lesson plans.

Good teachers know that the single greatest thing they can instill in their students is the desire to read.

Good teachers don't need a presidential commission to tell them what's wrong with America's public schools. The closest most of these "experts" get to a real classroom is when they fly over one on the way to Washington.

Good teachers wait a few seconds before they break up a fist fight in the corridor. Bad teachers turn heel and walk down a different corridor and hope that no one sees them.

Good teachers know that class rank is a sinister and official declaration that half the kids in the school are "below average." Bad teachers love to remind the slower kids just how low their class rank is.

Bad teachers think that higher salaries will turn them into good teachers. Good teachers know that as long as they choose to stay in the classroom they'll do the best job they can.

Good teachers don't have a spouse who also teaches. Or children who want to grow up to be teachers. Bad teachers want their children to grow up to be just like them.

Good teachers don't want or need tenure to protect their jobs.

the Good Teacher

Good teachers know that if they are not careful, someone might try to make them a vice principal.

Good teachers can eat their lunch in less than fifteen minutes, write with Bic pens, and raise their hands in restaurants. Bad teachers drink their milk with two straws; read *People* magazine in a supermarket line, but never buy one; believe in retirement; oppose any scheme to cut taxes; and safe from their own advice, advise others on how to get a job outside the classroom.

Good teachers know that the definition of cruel and unusual punishment is being required to attend any of the following events: a sports award banquet, a Memorial Day assembly in the gym (which is like having a Bar Mitzvah between the second and third innings of an Industrial League softball game), a pep rally (why do all cheerleaders sound exactly alike?), a September greeting from the principal ("It's amazing how fast the summer flies by"), and a staff meeting on "effective schools."

Good teachers aren't afraid to say where they went to college or what their SAT scores were.

Good teachers know that the only difference between the NEA and the Teamsters is the number of tattoos per capita. Bad teachers don't know that the NEA is a union.

Good teachers have the common sense not to take this list too seriously.

4 *How Not to Dress for School: A Story*

Some teachers believe that clothes are important. They argue that teachers have to look the part. Not me. I've spent the better part of my life honing down a fine indifference to clothes. By the time I discover what's "in," it's been "out" for months. Such impassiveness, of course, has spared me the embarrassment of owning a Nehru jacket.

If I ever had a fashion model, it would be Clarence Darrow. America's greatest criminal lawyer always looked as if he got dressed in a wind tunnel. Once, when he was asked about his disheveled appearance by a group of natty reporters, he said, "Why, boys, I buy clothes in the same shops you do. The only difference is that I sleep in mine."

Well, that's me. For years I survived nicely without owning a suit. One blue sport coat was enough. I'd wear it to the first day of school and then put it away until the next September. The rest of the time I wore slacks and a shirt. If I happened to sleep in them on occasion, so much the better.

Then, for some totally unexplainable reason, I bought a three-piece suit. It wasn't a conservative dark blue pin-striped suit, but a rather spectacular brown velvet suit. I didn't realize just how spectacular it was until I decided to wear it to school on a dare.

The minute I stepped foot in the school, I knew I was in for a long day. People didn't recognize me. Grizzly Adams had been transformed into Oscar Wilde. One woman teacher, after expressing her admiration for the suit, ran across me several times during the course of the day. Nothing unusual about that since it happened every day. But this day she was transfixed by the brown velvet. After several greetings, she finally stopped and said, "You see, I hardly ever noticed you before, now I'm seeing you everywhere."

The male teachers were less kind. They wanted to know what drunk I had rolled in what back alley. Some wanted to know if I'd lost a bet or something. Still others wondered aloud whether my suit would set back the union's request for higher salaries.

It was the kids, however, who were most shocked. I'd just written a newspaper article about my old VW Bug. In the article, which the students read, I wore my poverty on my sleeve. For example, I wrote that "I have worn my corduroy pants so long that they could have passed for chinos." And that "When my apartment was broken into, the thieves left the TV because they couldn't find the pliers they needed to change the channels."

One student, on seeing me in my brown velvet suit, came up and felt the sleeve. He then looked up at me and said, "Mr. Dewey, I've read your article and, you know, you just can't trust anyone anymore." So much for youth's idealism. Of course, the kid flunked. As for the suit, it has been retired. And it will remain retired until Vermont becomes America's leading exporter of fresh peaches and Maine clams.

5 *Advice to the First-Year Teacher*

Although I never thought about being a teacher when I was growing up, many people in my generation obviously did. But low pay, lower status, and the repetitious nature of the work drove many out of the profession after only a few years. Teaching is a unique job. It takes a great deal of dedication, inexhaustible enthusiasm, and a willingness to live on the brink of poverty for the first several years. Most young people who aspire to be teachers don't fully understand or appreciate the nature of the work when they first step in front of a classroom. So I strongly recommend that you avoid at all costs "dedicating your life" to teaching. Dedicate yourself to one year and let it go at that. The advantage is that you'll be able to keep your options open and you won't feel like a failure if you discover that teaching isn't your cup of oolong. Other things to keep in mind:

Share an apartment. You won't be able to afford a decent one on your own. But I suggest that you resist the natural temptation to live with another teacher. Find someone else so that you can maintain an open line to the outside world.

Keep your eyes open and your mouth shut in the faculty room. At least for the first month or so. You'll probably want a mentor during your first year, so it's important to find out who the yahoos are right off the bat. When you find someone who talks about something other than sports, food, or other teachers, then it's time to make friends.

Don't take graduate courses the first year. There are few jobs in this world that are tougher than being a first-year teacher, so don't complicate your life further by going to school at night. What you will need to do, however, is to read like crazy in whatever spare time you have. This is especially true of social studies and English teachers. Teaching is wonderful therapy for the recent college grad who thinks he or she already knows it all.

Sit in on other classes. Some teachers will object to your presence because they don't want anyone else (except the students, of course) to see what they really do. If you're there, they'll feel obligated to teach a full fifty minutes when ordinarily they would give the last fifteen minutes to the students to start their homework. Good teachers, on the other hand, will have no objections to having you in the room. Great teachers will invite you to sit in before you even get a chance to ask.

Don't worry about your classroom evaluations too much. Remember, you're only committed for one year of teaching. And, in any event, most department chairpersons follow the teacher's code which says, "I'm OK, you're OK."

Remember that the people in front of you are just kids. Some first-year teachers like to strut their college training on some obscure subject before tenth-graders. The kids won't be impressed, they'll just be bored.

Avoid the front office as much as possible. Principals have a way of nabbing first-year teachers who just happen to be in the area to supervise the extracurricular activities that no one else wants to supervise. My advice is to find out quickly what clubs need a faculty advisor and pick the one *you* like.

Live in the town where you teach. If you're going to teach, you might as well go for the whole experience.

live in the town where you teach

6 *Radicals and Reactionaries*

America's public school policy is fair game for all the kooks and right-wingers in this country. The two extremes agree only that the present way of doing things stinks and that they have the right answers for educating our children. The poor educational moderate is caught in the crossfire. One side thinks that he is an insensitive boob while the other side thinks he is a mollycoddling wimp who should try working for a living.

Take busing, for example. The moderate advocates limited busing as a last resort to achieve some form of racial balance in the schools. The radical favors busing all students according to their *political* beliefs. All kids whose parents belong to the NRA would go to one school somewhere off the coast while all the kids whose parents support the ACLU would go to another school. The reactionary also favors busing, but his busing would be based on *religious* beliefs. Any student who believes that the fatal flaw in the school prayer debate is that there is no God would go to one school to review Thomas Aquinas. All God-fearing Christians would go to another

the Radical

school and their parents would be able to take a tax credit on
school lunches.

In the radical's ideal school, Stalin's purges of the 1930's
would be skipped over. In the reactionary's ideal school, Voltaire and the Enlightenment would get the ax. The radical
wouldn't let his kids read *None Dare Call It Treason* or *The
National Review*. The reactionary wouldn't let the students
read *The New York Times* or watch CBS. The radical, always
a true believer in affective learning, would require the ritual
hugging of all freshpersons (a.k.a. ninth-graders) and one hour
of TM every day. The reactionary, always a true believer in
the curative powers of corporal punishment, would require
the ritual flogging of all freshmen and one hour each day of
close-order drill. The radical would make Norman Thomas's

26

birthday a holiday while the reactionary would give the kids the day off on Whittaker Chambers's birthday.

The radical would make *Our Bodies, Ourselves* required summer reading while the reactionary would insist that the kids read the John Birch Society's *Blue Book.* In a school run by the radicals, the kids would be asked to plan each class for themselves and the teachers would suspend any kid who dared to ask, "Do we have to do whatever we want today?"

the Reactionary

In a school run by the reactionaries, the students would begin *each class* with a prayer and the teachers would suspend any kid who asks to go to the bathroom. The radical's definition of the three R's is rapture, revelry, and revolution. The reactionary's definition of the three R's is ritual, rectitude, and reverence.

Well, the educational moderate can take comfort in the fact that the bark of both fringe groups is worse than their bite. Most radicals and reactionaries don't become teachers and, if they do, they don't last very long. Teaching is a middle-of-the-road, conformist occupation ill-suited to those who would jump out of the chorus line of middle America.

If you're curious as to where you might stand along the educational spectrum, I invite you to write your own report on education. Here's how to do it. Just read the selection below, then circle the words you like best. Send the results to your local newspaper as a letter to the editor. If you get attacked by the local NEA president then you're probably a reactionary because the NEA just doesn't attack radicals. The NEA usually responds to left-wing criticism by saying something like, "Yes, we know, but with the Republicans in control, it's just not possible." If an angry response to your letter comes from the commander of the American Legion, then you're probably a radical. If no one responds to your letter, it's because the people in your town haven't yet learned to read. Ready?

> Education in (America, our state, our jerkwater town, Ms. Walter's class) is in a state (of chaos, of free expression, of dyspepsia, called Maine) because it is controlled by (liberals, Fascists, the senior class, the Gay Faculty Alliance). For the past twenty years SAT scores have fallen faster than (a Diebold safe, the Italian lira, Ronald Reagan's cheeks, a

boy's voice during puberty). The kids today don't even know how to (salute the flag, foxtrot, take their hats off in church, score a string of bowling). All they want to do is (roll funny cigarettes, carry huge radios down the street, wear obscene T-shirts, get into business school). And the (person, creep, moron, windbag) at the front of the room isn't any bargain either. The teachers are all (underworked, overpaid, unclean, unappreciated). Frankly, I think most teachers are nothing but a pack of (communists, freeloaders, pederasts, Camels). If we really want to reform our schools the first thing we have to do is to (bus half the teachers to Poland, make Charles Bronson the vice principal, nuke the English department, bring "Our Miss Brooks" out of retirement.)

7 *Student Styles*

THE PET ROCK

If the Pet Rock were a can of peas, he would carry a generic label. A utility-grade student, the Pet Rock lets everything wash over his head. In June the Pet Rock knows exactly as much as he knew in September. Like his nearest relative, the real rock, the Pet Rock is well disciplined, easily overlooked, and hard to motivate. The Pet Rock loves multiple choice exams and movies with lots of action. He prefers war movies, but will take any movie so long as people move about. On the other hand, the Pet Rock would rather do almost anything else than watch a filmstrip.

THE PREPPIE

The Preppie is everything the Pet Rock isn't. The Preppie knows how important it is to please the teacher. She would bite her tongue before she would correct a teacher's spelling

the Preppie

error on the blackboard. Grades are vital to the Preppie. She is the only student who will demand that the A– be changed to a straight A. The Preppie will also demand that she get an A for completing the simplest worksheet rather than the standard check mark. The Preppie values the mommy who can write research papers and knows how to disguise cleverly her plagiarism.

THE MUNCHKIN

The Munchkin is a cousin to the Pet Rock, but she has more life. The Munchkin loves to wash the blackboard and collate papers for the teacher. During a teacher strike, the Munchkin will join the picket line. The Munchkin does all her homework, takes notes religiously, and comes in for extra help every night. She rarely passes a test but survives nicely on her social skills. Only a Munchkin would tell a brand-new substitute teacher her real name. The Munchkin is the most likely in her class to be elected to Congress.

THE JOHN WAYNE

Now here is a really sick puppy. The poor John Wayne of the 1980's is growing up in a generation without a war to fight. But he brings his equipment to school every day anyway. He wears fatigue pants, a web belt complete with canteen, and he thinks that Che Guevara works for Calvin Klein. He uses a knapsack to carry his books. War, of course, is the only subject that interests him and he can talk about that all day long. The major historical hate figure of the John Wayne is Harry Truman. Why? Because Harry didn't have the guts to nuke the Russians when we had a monopoly in atomic weapons. The John Wayne's idea of survival training is to lock a freshman who weighs less than one hundred pounds in a wall locker. Bomb scares and false alarms keep the John Wayne coming back to school. When not in the classroom, the John Wayne can be seen at night conducting war game exercises on the municipal golf course.

THE ERASMUS

Erasmus, the 16th century humanist, was so brilliant his teachers asked him to add comments to his papers so that they could figure out what he was talking about. The Erasmus is still around. This kid knows more than most of her teachers. Teachers read the homework of the Erasmus not so much to grade it, but to learn from it. Teachers can safely use the Erasmus's test as their answer key. Before a teacher dares to correct the Erasmus, he checks at least three outside sources. I've had maybe three or four students like that over the years. Whenever the Erasmus gave an incorrect answer I always double-checked the question to see if it was in any way misleading.

THE NEMESIS

The Nemesis is the school thug. The Nemesis screams when he thinks his rights are being violated but couldn't care less about anyone else's rights. The Nemesis loves to beat up on kids half his size. He's the kid you assign to the last seat in the last row and hope that he falls asleep. It's either that or you put him in the front seat of the middle row and try to buddy up to him. You never, never ask the Nemesis to read out loud in class nor do you question how the obscene comments got into his textbook. The Nemesis is the most likely member of his class to get elected to the school board a few years down the road.

THE SHADOW

The Shadow is the student who dropped out of school months ago, but the school still carries him or her on the attendance rolls. I know several Shadows who were living west of the Mississippi but were still appearing on the daily attendance sheet in a Massachusetts school. All schools, of course, have the Shadow or Shadows. The more kids you claim, the more state aid your school gets. In some urban schools 20 percent of the student body are Shadows.

THE PANIC BUTTON

The Panic Button gets a hernia from just looking at a test. No matter how well prepared the kid is the night before, the sight of that bluebook causes heart palpitations. An experienced teacher can spot the Panic Button five rows away by his open mouth and his glazed-over eyes. The Panic Button scores in the low 300's on his SATs and marries the first girl he dates. Still, there's potential in the Panic Button and, when he overcomes his nervousness, he does quite well as an adult. The Panic Button often arrives at his twenty-fifth reunion in a Jaguar.

THE JOCKSTRAP

In the case of the Jockstrap, all of God's gifts are bestowed from the neck down. The Jockstrap tries hard to imitate big leaguers on and off the field. He wears his gym shorts over his sweat pants. Entertainment to the Jockstrap is spending his free time playing hockey with an empty milk carton in the cafeteria after school. He is the only student to score lower than the Panic Button on the SATs. But colleges tend to overlook that if the kid can break heads inside a football helmet.

the Jockstrap

HAROLD

I've never subscribed to the theory that there is no such thing as a bad kid. There are plenty of them. I just don't happen to believe that there is such a thing as a bad kid named

Harold. All the Harolds I have known have been like little old men. Wise and temperate beyond their years, the Harolds talk to you like a person rather than a teacher. All the other adolescents need about ten more years to get where Harold is at seventeen.

THE BAD SEED

If you remember the movie, you'll know what I mean. It is always the Bad Seed who suggests that you have unnatural sex with yourself. The male Bad Seed uses the blade of a knife to guide his eyes while reading. The female Bad Seed writes naughty words (that she can't spell) on walls. The Bad Seed of either sex pays for lunch with a fifty-dollar bill.

THE IDEAL GRADUATE

The school has done a decent job if the graduates know when to use contraceptives, which side the CIA is really on, and the actual odds of hitting a state lottery. The Ideal Graduate also knows not to smoke, that spontaneous human combustion is for real, how lucky an American is in the grand scheme of things, and the difference between free speech and gossip. But the sine qua non of the Ideal Graduate is whether he or she can properly bait a fishhook and knows the difference between probate and a rebate.

8 Grading the Students: A Report Card

If the Bureau of the Census can come up with a profile of the average American, I suppose I can come up with a report card that reflects the average high school student today. I haven't seen every student to attend high school in America over the last decade and a half; it just seems that way. Please be reminded that any resemblance to any student—living or dead—is purely coincidental.

Intestinal Fortitude: C–

Without question, this is the generation of the Hostess Twinkee. Soft on the outside, soft on the inside. The average suburban student doesn't have to fight for anything more serious than a place in the lunch line. An extra homework assignment is reason enough for a temper tantrum. There are, of course, exceptions. Some kids do crave risks that make their parents cringe. But for the overfed majority, whining and dining are challenge enough.

Knowledge of Anatomy: A+

Some things never change. Teenage boys still line up to

read the swimsuit issue of *Sports Illustrated* in the school's library. By the time I get to it, the drool has made it impossible to separate the pages. This was once an X-rated, adult category. (When I was in high school, and in search of a cheap thrill, I had to wade through one of Boccaccio's ribald tales or check out the lingerie ads in women's magazines.) No more. Today the kids paste the inside of their lockers with photos from *Penthouse* or *Playgirl*. So the A+ for anatomy is well deserved.

Sense of Humor: C+

Given their ages, there is still hope. Slapstick is a bigger hit than anything remotely subtle. Kids loved the shower scene from *Porky's*. Of course, if a freshman "loses his lunch" in the corridor, it's guaranteed howls. And if a teacher should happen to slip in it, they would have to call off school. With puberty, boys rediscover tits. (But now they don't belong to mommy.) Any tits will do. The bigger the better. So during school "spirit week," guys in drag always have incredibly huge knockers. And everyone slaps their knees at this demonstration of first-class wit and imagination.

Geography: D+

Not to be confused with anatomy. Most students think you need a passport to visit a neighboring state. TV puts the world at your fingertips, so why study maps? There is outer space and the living room, but little in between. Maybe it's something in the food, but after ten weeks I've had freshmen who still couldn't find their lockers.

The Written Word: D

The combined effects of TV, the telephone, and video games have destroyed the average kid's ability to write even a post card home from summer camp asking for more money. On the positive side, poor writing might reduce the number of bank robberies. What's a female teller to think if she is handed a note that reads, "This is a stuck-up?" She just might haul off and deck the stupid twit.

Current Events: C–

Most students can't tell the difference between a news flash and a hot flash. No matter. Today's current event is tomorrow's history and the students aren't going to remember that either.

Idealism: C

Have students gone to San Francisco with flowers in their hair recently? Money and the pursuit of still more money have left love beads and communal grass in the dust.

Honesty: B

Kids don't cheat on tests much anymore. Or at least they're not getting caught as much. One reason for this is that kids don't seem to care as much as they once did. The competitive struggle to get into college has vanished. Top-notch colleges can still pick and choose, but every street-wise adolescent knows that higher education has become a buyer's market. Colleges pay bounties to students who can recruit kids from their home towns to sign up for four years at Upper Creek State College. No matter how bad their academic record or how low the SAT scores, there's some college somewhere waiting to take their money. Slow learners and delinquent types don't have to cheat. They know that if they just hang around long enough, they'll get their diplomas and admission to some college if they want it.

Appearance: B–

Public schools have gone casual. Coats and ties are unusual even for some teachers. But dirt, as a form of social protest

the style is casual

or simply as a manifestation of bad training, has been out of style for some time now. The lice squad has been retired along with truant officers. The dress code has disappeared under the combined heat of court decisions and faculty acquiescence. I regard this as progress. Young ladies in flimsy spring clothes and obscene T-shirts are the only major distractions.

U.S. History: C+

This is a tough one. If we talk only about the grasp students in general have of the causes of, say, the Civil War or the Depression, the students would earn only a C-. But when you add in an A for knowledge of the Bill of Rights and the Warren Court decisions, the picture changes somewhat. Every kid is a reincarnated Clarence Darrow. They know what they can get away with and what they can't. And they know the rules of evidence. They have developed a finely tuned sense of injustice. If there is even the slightest weakness in the teacher's case against some miscreant, there will be a dozen public defenders leaping to the accused's side.

Language: D-

Let's face it, we all use the language but most of us vary it a little. Teenagers have reduced the art of conversation to rearranging the same five hundred words. Complete sentences, unspiced with barnyard expletives, are rare. Girls have achieved total equality with boys in this regard.

Health: F

Kids are indestructible. Or so they believe. Some with an A in chemistry continue to consume dangerous amounts of liquor, drugs, and tobacco. Educational reformers lament that the schools don't teach anything of practical use. Well, in the past ten years we have seen a veritable tidal wave of information on drugs. Yet students continue to consume.

9 *Morons and Malaprops*

We all know that the pay isn't great, but teachers do get their share of free laughs. Despite rumors to the contrary, the classroom can be a funny place. I suppose it has something to do with the combination of high purpose and stupidity and the nature of suppressed laughter. In any event, here are some of the laughs I've come across as a teacher.

I once made the perfectly innocent mistake of asking a United States history class, "Who was Peggy Eaton?" Well, the straight answer is that she was the wife of the Secretary of War during Andrew Jackson's administration and was involved in a bit of a social scandal. Unfortunately, well . . . you know the rest.

I wish I had a nickel for every student who has claimed that Michelangelo painted the "Sixteenth Chapel."

Where else, but in the classroom, would you discover that Henry David Thoreau wrote *On Golden Pond*?

I remember asking a kid to write an essay on a heavyweight championship fight. I then learned that the defeated challenger's handlers conceded defeat by "throwing in the toilet."

You would think that by the time a kid got to high school, he or she would know something about the Constitution and the first ten amendments. But when I asked a student to identify just one of the first ten amendments, he said, "You can't do it to your neighbor's wife."

I know now why Clark was so willing to spend two years in the woods exploring the Louisiana Purchase under orders from President Jefferson. He went with Lois.

In Hemingway's *The Old Man and the Sea* there is a part about the old man having a recurring dream about lions on the beach. When I asked a question about the old man's dream, one student wrote, "The old man was dreaming of *loins* on the beach." I gave the kid full credit because I was having the same recurring dream myself.

Where else but on a history test would you find out that Julius and Ethel Rosenberg were *convinced* of conspiracy?

Once I gave an exam which required that the students use a 2H pencil to mark their answer sheets. When I asked one student if she had brought a 2H pencil, she apologized and said, "I'm sorry, I only brought one."

Of course, teachers make their own gaffes. I recall being a study-hall teacher besieged with student requests to go to the bathroom. As soon as one student returned, another would ask to go to the bathroom. As soon as that student returned, another student would ask. After five or six such requests my patience was gone. Finally, when a girl made yet another powder room request, I had reached the end of my rope. In exasperation I said, "OK, you can go but you're the last one. I don't want a *steady stream.* " For once in my teaching career everyone in the room got the joke at once. We all laughed continuously until the bell rang twenty minutes later.

Sometimes the student turns the intellectual tables on the teacher. Once, when I was teaching in the eighth grade in Vermont, I tried to illustrate how difficult kids find it to compute simple everyday math problems. In the age of the pocket calculator it seems that many students have lost the ability to do mental calculations. To drive the point home, I asked the students to figure out a taxi fare.

You know the kind of problem, so much for the first quarter mile and then so much for every half mile thereafter. The correct answer was $7. Most students got the wrong answer. One student's guess was $5. To dramatize the practical consequences of such an error, I asked the student, "What would you do if the cabbie on this $7 ride was a three-hundred-pound gorilla and you had only your $5?" After a moment's reflection, the kid replied, "I'd have him back up $2 worth!" From that point on, I ceased to worry about his future in this world.

Then there was the time when I was teaching European history. The subject for a couple of days had been Voltaire, the great French writer and social critic. In my summary I wanted to talk about his monumental achievements against superstitions and falsehoods and the fact that the demons he crushed no longer concern people very much.

But somewhere between *Candide* and Voltaire's run-in with Frederick the Great of Prussia, I got derailed and began to talk about Vietnam. When I finally got back on track the next day, I asked the students why Voltaire isn't studied much anymore. One resident wit suggested, "It's because you keep talking about your war experiences in Vietnam!"

I recall asking this question on a test: "In what country was the battle of Borodino _____?" One student completed my incomplete sentence by adding "fought."

And another outstanding master of repartee couldn't remember that St. Helena was Napoleon's final island of exile. Instead of leaving the space blank or taking a stab in the dark, she wrote in next to St. Helena, "Pray for me."

It was events like these that kept me in the classroom long after selling insurance began to look good.

10   *Love between Periods*

"I don't believe virginity's as common as it used to be," sang Don Williams in his hit song a few years ago. Well, I think Don might be on to something. The way things are going a virgin has about as much chance of getting through high school intact as a camel has of passing through the eye of a needle. The peer pressure to lower your shorts and commingle is almost unbearable. The plain truth is that the body is screaming, "Oh, yes, please do it," while the thin-lipped, know-better elders are saying, "You do and I'll smack you one!"

It has always been this way once the kid passes puberty. One solution is to marry young. In many present-day cultures, eighteen-year-olds have already been married for four years and are raising families of their own. Parents rush their daughters to the altar at the onset of puberty to prevent an untimely deflowering.

In America, however, we try to keep adolescents in a state of suspended sexuality. It is a noble cause and I would like to help in any way I can. Here are my thoughts on some preventive steps that, if taken, just might keep those zippers zipped a little longer.

45

1. Reverse those good health habits. Forget the good food, the daily vitamins and the regular exercise. These only make the kids more robust. And horny.

2. Shorten the passage time between classes from five minutes to thirty seconds. There might be a few more accidents, but not the kind that embarrass parents and school officials. Kids who sleep with their eyes open in class are instantly transformed into finely tuned athletes as soon as the bell rings at the end of the period. Five minutes isn't much time to get it on, but the kids try anyway. It usually happens near the boiler room. There's a boy and a girl in close embrace. And only one foot out of four is on the floor.

3. Bring back saltpeter and mashed potatoes.

4. Purge all reading materials about virgins being tossed into volcanoes. It's bad publicity if you're trying to sell virginity. Virgins need to become the new literary heroes. They must always come out on top, so to speak.

5. Institute a new busing program. Forget the preaching and sermons. Separation works better than inspiration. So bus all boys west of the Mississippi and all girls east of the Mississippi. Then guard the damn river.

6. Continue to encourage the development of smaller cars and bucket seats. The rate of sexual activity between teenagers is directly proportional to the size of the car seats. Latin Americans still have an explosive birthrate because they're still driving '57 Chevys.

7. Insist the male athletes play *without* protective gear. Especially football and hockey players. Even the most hardy males will sing a different tune after a well-aimed slapshot or blind-side tackle.

8. Make all boys get crew cuts. Girls will spend all their time rubbing boys' heads and telling them how cute they look.

9. Outlaw sweaters for girls. Bib overalls and a Pendleton shirt should be the required uniform. (This is not likely to be

effective for long. After all, it's not the wrapping but the package that counts.)

love between the periods

11 Win, Place, and Showoff: A Chapter on Parents

It's not easy being a parent. And not every parent is responsible if one of the little things grows up to be Jack the Ripper. That said, parents still do some pretty weird things to muck up their children. For example:

The parent whose son gets into every school but Harvard and then says, "My son didn't finish second, he struck out!"

The mother who calls her two-hundred-pound son out of class to give him the lunch he forgot to take in the morning.

The parents who put every little achievement of their son or daughter in the local newspaper.

The father who goes to all of his son's football games and none of his daughter's field hockey games.

The parents who tell their children how much they hated school when they were kids. (Enough young people learn to hate school all by themselves, thank you.)

The parents who insist that their illiterate children take all honors-level courses.

The parents who have a trophy room built for their kids.

The parents who do their children's homework for them.

Or worse, the mother who types all her kid's papers.

The parents who constantly write "sick" notes to get their kid out of gym class.

The parents who insist that their children say grace before eating their lunch in the school cafeteria.

The parents who keep switching their kids from public school to private school and back again.

The parents who tell their kids that "Teachers should get an honest job."

The parent who tells his son to apologize to the teacher for some moral outrage and then says, "Remember, son, you can't beat city hall!"

Here are some of the more memorable types of parents I met while teaching:

SUPERDAD

The twenty-four-hour store of parents. Available all the time. Half the kids think he's one of the teachers. On the coldest, rainiest day in November, he's the only one watching the girls' field hockey game. The only problem with Superdad is what to do with him when the school day is over. Doesn't this guy have a home?

THE WEEPING MADONNA

This mother has a son who is being crucified by his teachers. And all because he pulled one knife on one teacher. How is her son going to get into the state university if the school insists on sending his police record along with his transcript? The Weeping Madonna can plead for hours about how this is her only son or her last son. (To which I can only say, "Thank God.")

THE SPACE SHOT

Or the Air Head. It's hard to raise kids when you're still in your own puberty crisis. The Space Shot is a product of the sixties who swore she would never have kids, but did anyway. She's still waiting to hitch a ride to San Francisco long after the flowers in her hair have wilted. The Space Shot lives on the husband-a-month plan and decries the schools for not teaching values.

THE ABSENTEE LANDLORD

Last seen heading for Florida with his new girlfriend. The Absentee Landlord figures that when his children reach the age of ten, they're the school's problem. Sends a postcard for Christmas. The one thing the Absentee Landlord tells his kids for guidance is that he didn't like school either.

THE BIBLE BELTER

The Bible Belter inspects every book for the slightest hint of immorality or unpatriotic bias. The Bible Belter would ban all books not published by the Liberty Mountain Press or the John Birch Society. This type of parent thinks that the lotus of the cow[1] is a prime rib. He also thinks that Wounded Knee is a football injury.

THE RUBBER STAMP

There aren't many Rubber Stamps left. They have been largely replaced by the Veto who rejects anything and every-

[1] See the Kama Sutra.

thing the schools try to do. With the Rubber Stamp, however, whatever the teacher says goes. The Rubber Stamp often never went beyond grammar school and still thinks that teachers are pretty swell people. With every other parent type the kid is innocent until proven guilty. With the Rubber Stamp it's just the other way around.

THE FIXER

The Fixer pays more in property taxes than most teachers make in yearly salary. The Fixer sends his kid to public school because he thinks public school teachers and administrators are easy to manipulate. This parent would pull all the strings to get his daughter the lead in the spring musical. He gets elected to the school board just so he can better harass his daughter's teachers.

the Fixer

12 A Brief Look at Those Educational Reports

The trouble with most studies on education is that they are written by a committee. The only really good book ever written by a committee was the King James Version of the Bible. The committee writers of the world should have quit while they were ahead. But, of course, they didn't. Concern over America's public schools got committee lovers flocking like Japanese beetles in heat. The result was a dozen or so reports on education. *A Nation at Risk: The Imperative for Educational Reform,* for example, was written by eighteen people. *High School: A Report on Secondary Education in America* had twenty-eight contributors. And *Academic Preparation for College: What Students Need to Know and Be Able to Do* had two hundred authors. The result was a literary disaster.

The reports all have subtitles because a simple title is never adequate. And do the writers ever love hyperbole and pyrotechnics! A clear, honest report on the state of American education would have been too dull for most people to read. So the studies had to be juiced up with memorable quotes.

That's the only way to make the cover of *Time* or *Newsweek*. *A Nation at Risk* got the most national attention. No wonder. It tells you, "Our nation is at risk. The educational foundations of our society are being eroded by a rising tide of mediocrity that threatens our future as a nation and a people. . . . If an unfriendly foreign power had attempted to impose on America the mediocre educational performance that exists today, we might well have viewed it as an act of war." When I read that, my first instinct was to call out the Marines. When I went on to read, "We have in effect been committing an act of unthinking unilateral educational disarmament," I wanted to lock up every public-school teacher in a soccer stadium the way they do it in South America. The committee writers were probably the same people who poked fun at Jimmy Carter for saying that the energy crisis was "the moral equivalent of war."

In the face of this national catastrophe, what does the National Committee on Excellence in Education, which produced *A Nation at Risk*, recommend? A total restructuring of American schools? Not a chance. The public schools are turning our kids' brains into sewer gas and they recommend more of the same. More homework, longer days, and a longer school year. They must be working on the assumption that it's impossible to get too much of a bad thing. Not once did the commission members acknowledge that there's nothing you can do about Monday mornings or Friday afternoons so long as we continue to view "education" as a five-days-a-week obligation and as something the school does to the kid.

The National Committee does take credit for reinventing the wheel, however. It identifies the five *new* basics: English, mathematics, science, social studies, and computer science. Just think, it took eighteen people a year and a half to tell us what every fool already knows. The National Committee goes on to recommend higher salaries for teachers, stronger discipline, tougher standards, and better teachers. Now where have I read that before?

Well, if you don't count anything published between, say, the turn of the century and 1983, I suppose it would have to have been in *Action for Excellence: A Comprehensive Plan to Improve Our Nation's Schools,* produced by the National Task Force on Education for Economic Growth. This task force (again, note the military terminology) suggests some mind-boggling new ideas. The task force, for example, thinks that the state should develop plans for improving education; that the federal government should continue to support education; that school systems should establish firm discipline; that schools should strengthen their curriculum; that student progress should be measured through periodic tests; and that schools should challenge gifted students. Pretty heady stuff, huh?

Of course, if any commission has some sharp cookies in it, they'll recommend that further research and study be done. Such is the case with *America's Competitive Challenge: The Need for a National Response.* This sixteen-member task force, set up by the Business-Higher Education Forum, recommends that the President of the United States appoint a national commission of industrial competitiveness, a presidential advisor on economic competitiveness, and an information center on international competitiveness. It's nice work if you can get it. I will give this commission some credit. Besides a bunch of little ones, they make only one overall recommendation: "As a nation, we must develop a consensus that industrial competitiveness is crucial to our social and economic well-being. Such a consensus will require a shift in public attitudes about national priorities, as well as changes in public perceptions about the nature of our economic malaise." (Is that you again, Jimmy?)

Sometimes you have to wonder about the minimum competency of the people who write these reports. *In High School: A Report on Secondary Education in America,* the authors refer to teachers as "being credentialed." That's an example of a decent middle-class noun getting mugged until it becomes a verb. And in *Making the Grade,* a report sponsored by the Twentieth Century Fund, we find this gem: "The difficulties of coping with these burdens have been compounded in some cities by inappropriate judicial intervention and by the spread of the trade-union mentality that has accompanied the bureaucratization and politicization of the schools." I sure hope that the eleven members of this committee never get a chance to write for children.

These reformers all want the school to be all things to all people. But it isn't easy to put English, history, math, science, home economics, industrial arts, foreign language, career education, computer literacy, sex education, drug counseling, gym, driver education, library science, consumer education, extracurricular activities, saluting the flag, going to the bathroom, making out in the corridors, and eating lunch into a seven-hour day. All any school really needs are kids who want to learn, teachers who know how to teach with fire in their eyes, community support, and strong local funding.

13 The Dewey Plan for School Reform

Just so you don't think I'm a nattering nabob of negativism, I do have a concrete plan for the survival of the public school. It's a package deal. I'm not responsible if your school implements only part of the Dewey Plan for School Reform. It's all or nothing.

Use the high-school prom method of teaching. I've never been much of a fan of the high-school prom. (I was cajoled into taking a junior girl I didn't even know to my senior prom and then she almost wrecked my father's car when I let her drive.) Still, a decent prom always has a theme. It could be the South Sea Islands or April in Paris or Shangri-La, but there is always a theme. My godfather, the sainted John Dewey, used to recommend that every elementary grade have its own theme around which to focus the curriculum. The fourth-grade theme, for example, might be boats. The kids would study everything there is to study about boats from design to famous voyages to sea stories. From this study of boats the kids would learn their math, English, history, geography, and so forth.

Now I suggest that we extend this principle to secondary schools. The entire ninth-grade curriculum, for example, could center on the theme of the human body. What kid would not look forward to the end of the summer vacation if he or she were going back to school to spend a whole year studying the human body? All the so-called basic subjects would still be taught, only the theme would be the human body. History classes could cover how nature and humans have conspired to destroy the body by studying such subjects as the Black Plague, the 1919 influenza epidemic, and Hiroshima. Art classes could study Michelangelo's sketches for the Sistine Chapel and the facial expressions of Ben Shahn drawings. Instead of a foreign language the kids could study body language and learn when to cross their legs and when not to cross their legs. And, of course, all English students would be required to read *Fanny Hill*, Boccaccio's *Decameron*, and *The Joy of Sex*.

Return the inkwells to the classroom. The ideal way to build a school would be first to locate where you want to put the inkwells and then build the school around them. With an inkwell, the kids couldn't claim that their ballpoint pens have run out of ink in the middle of a major exam. And the inkwell would return a touch of class to the school desk. What style and grace is there in "flicking your Bic?" (Of course, the ultimate reform would be to bring back the quill, but first things first.)

Remove all the clocks. Clocks are anathema to teaching. Teachers look at them and kids look at them. And they're all thinking the same thing: "How much longer do I have to be here?" Like Pavlovian dogs, the kids begin panting five minutes before the bell is supposed to ring. They start scratching their sneakers along the floor, like greyhounds waiting for the mechanical rabbit. They can smell the scent of the hallway and freedom. The big-name reformers can talk all they want about the classics and computer literacy, but I say the most important reform would be to throw every damn clock out the window.

Cancel the eighth grade. Just eliminate it. Like the thirteenth floor in a thirty-story building. Eighth graders aren't good for themselves and they aren't good for the school. It's their crisis year and they ought to keep it to themselves. Send them on an "Outward Bound" project to Tibet or let them work on a Norwegian freighter. Send them anywhere but school.

If you can't find the political support to eliminate the eighth grade, at least eliminate the requirement for American history that year. The same course is repeated in the eleventh grade anyway. Nothing drives a high-school history teacher up the wall more than hearing students complain, "We've had all this stuff before." The fact that they don't remember any of their eighth-grade history is irrelevent. The important thing is that the students are initially turned off to the subject. How many times do they have to land at Plymouth Rock? In place of the eighth-grade American history course, teach a reading development course called "Biographies." The kids have to develop an interest in people before they can develop an interest in history.

Close the teachers' lounge. As a general rule, whatever is good in life can't be done in school. Except in the teachers' lounge. There teachers can smoke, drink coffee, tell gross jokes, swear, and generally comport themselves as adults. No fair. Such an enclave should not be allowed. There should be no "rest and recreation" at the front. Teachers should be required to eat with the kids. In the teachers' lounge, they can easily develop a "bomb shelter" mentality. A full-scale riot could be taking place just outside the door and you'll hear teachers mutter to each other, "Thank God I'm not out there."

Shrink the size of the classroom. This would go a long way towards solving the problem of declining enrollments. The real problem isn't numerical. It's optical. The classrooms are simply too big. Most were built during the baby boom of the fifties and sixties. They were designed to handle more than forty students. All you have to do now is to bring in the walls and create the illusion of the packed classroom. A properly designed room will make twenty students look like thirty-five. The room should be long and narrow rather than short and wide. It's the application of the elementary principle of the conservation of volume.

Nail down the desks again. The decline of public education began the day they unmoored the desks. Desks became a relative concept rather than an absolute. The classroom was reduced to a movable feast of mischief. Each teacher has his or her own idea on how the desks should be arranged. And so do the kids.

Enroll parents in classes. Then put them on potty patrol during their free periods. They will soon realize that the light at the end of the boys' bathroom will usually be followed by smoke and a funny smell. And the parents will have a chance to overhear a few restroom conversations, see the contents of a few wall lockers, and read some of the desk graffiti. That should spare some teachers from hearing incredulous parents defending their offspring with, "My kid wouldn't do anything like that!" At worst, this idea would keep parents off the streets.

Fire the best teachers. Yes, fire, not hire. It's really the only sensible thing to do. The best teachers are the ones who are most likely to succeed at another occupation. The weaker ones might have some difficulty and be a burden on society. And it's quite possible that the fired teachers will thank you in a year or two for doing them a favor. In any event, such a move would precipitate the kind of crisis public education needs if it is to get its act together again.

Make the kids buy their textbooks. Few things in this life have a shorter life expectancy than a school textbook. I've seen kids use Dickens's *The Tale of Two Cities* as an impromptu hockey puck in the cafeteria after school. I've seen kids use their thousand-page United States history texts as weapons. And I've read all the graffiti that makes the average textbook look like a New York subway after one year's use.

So make the kids pay for what they would destroy. In the long run it would save everyone money. The kids could sell their books to the kids in the class behind them. Or, even better, the school's business department could run its own used bookstore. Then the school could get rid of the typical school store which features little more than chewing gum, candy, and rock and roll T-shirts.

Build outhouses for all smokers. Indoor plumbing has done more to set back the cause of education and advance the interests of the tobacco lobby than anything I can think of. If students and teachers insist on smoking when they go to the john, then let them have their own separate buildings. That way the non-smokers won't have to choose between lung cancer and constipation.

Abolish the summer vacation. And replace it with a winter vacation. This would be a logical move to save money spent on heating the building during the winter. During the summer months you could begin school much earlier in the morning and be out before the real heat of the afternoon hits. More importantly, this plan would free the beaches from teenagers so that we older folks can enjoy our time in the sun uninterrupted by the beat of cassette players and the panting of pubescence.

Eliminate the cursive Q. Few things have done more to retard the cause of literacy than the existence of the letter *Q*. I know fewer than five people who can actually write an upper case cursive *Q*. I think they invented the typewriter just to help people avoid the embarrassment caused by not knowing how to write a proper cursive *Q*. It is supposed to look something like the number "2" but nobody seems to know for sure. Most people just make a circle with a sick little line cutting through the bottom. The letter *Q* is also a parasite. It can't exist without the help of a "u". The mere presence of such a letter undercuts the American value of self-sufficiency. So goodbye, John Q. Public, and hello John (anything but *Q*) Public.

Make sabbaticals mandatory. The best kind of curriculum has already been tried and consigned to the trash heap of history. The medieval guilds were right on the money when they matched the eager apprentice with the patient master in a one-to-one relationship over a long period of time. The apprentice learned everything the master knew from start to finish. Proof of achievement was furnished by the production of a "masterpiece." Unfortunately, that one-to-one relationship is rare in public schools. Today's teachers, for the most part, don't do what they teach: English teachers don't write or edit manuscripts, science teachers don't do research, and business teachers aren't in business. So what the kids get is secondhand, largely textbook knowledge. And that's too bad. That's why automatic and mandatory sabbaticals or leaves of absence must be given to teachers. Require them to take off for a year and do some of the things that they teach. Then, when they return to the school, assign these teachers to specific students who show interest in the same field of endeavor. This might even save the school some money since you could eliminate half the guidance department.

Dewey's Dream School. Like the medieval guild model, this one will never be adopted, but I thought you might like to hear it anyway. My idea is to take eight to ten kids and load them on a bus with two or three teachers who are well-versed in all subjects. Then let them tour Central and South America for the next four years with the summers off for home visits. The teachers would cover all the traditional subjects, but the kids would also be exposed to different languages, different cultures, and different ways of doing things. And if any of the kids become delinquent, you wouldn't have to send them to the vice principal's office. You could just drop them off by the side of the road and let them wait for the first terrorist or freedom fighter to come along.

Put the kids at risk. The bus tour idea would certainly put the kids at risk, but you don't have to go to such extreme lengths. Every good school should have adventure and risk-taking built into the curriculum. It could be a Project Adventure program or an Outward Bound program or any other scheme you can think of to induce the students to test their own limits. Even such simple things as writing a letter to the editor or conducting an interview with a public official can be high-risk propositions to some kids.

Make all teachers switch-hitters. Schools should require all teachers to be certified in two areas, not just one. There are several advantages to this proposal. For openers, a teacher could move from one subject to another to reduce the fatigue and boredom which eventually comes from teaching the same courses over and over again. For another, dual certification would tie the school together across departmental lines. And teachers with two areas of expertise would gain the respect and prestige which is so lacking today. Wouldn't it be great to have a school where the science teacher was also an English teacher? Or the social studies teacher was also a French teacher? Or, be still my heart, the phys ed teacher also taught advanced mathematics?

Adopt the Rainbow Coalition. Too often the so-called best schools are the lily-white schools in the wealthy suburbs. In a society which is rich with blacks, Asians, and Hispanics, it seems to me that a student at an all-white school would have a legal case against the local school board for intellectual and social deprivation. Every good school should be willing to do whatever is necessary to insure that it has at least some kind of racial and ethnic mix.

Keep the schools red. Here's another plea for tradition. Episcopal churches should be made of stone, baseball bats should be made of wood, and schools should be made of red brick.

the English (and Science) teacher

14 *Favorite Myths about Education*

As in any mass bureaucracy, whenever people in public education don't know what the hell is going on, they create another myth to fill the void. The thing that sets teachers apart from other public employees, however, is that they actually believe their own myths. They really believe, for example, that if the town spent 10 percent more on the public schools, the schools would show a 10 percent improvement. Every extra dollar spent, according to the myth, means one hundred pennies' worth of additional wisdom or knowledge. The same principle applies to class size. No one knows what the optimal class size is because there isn't one. But to hear some teachers tell it, the perfect class size is always smaller than the one they've got. I know one high-school teacher who, with only three classes and fifty self-motivated, self-teaching honors students, was barely able to keep his head above water. Other teachers, with five or six classes and 120 so-so students, somehow managed to do just fine. Following are some of my other favorite myths.

The best schools are in the suburbs. At first blush the people who believe this seem to be on to something. The schools in the suburbs are generally free of graffiti, the lawns get mowed, and the windows don't need wire mesh. The kids still have all their teeth and, for the most part, they cover their books when the teachers ask. But step inside most suburban schools and one thing hits you right away. Where are the black kids? Or the Chicanos or the Native Americans or the Puerto Ricans? Well, there aren't any. I taught at one suburban school that was so free of blacks, a white kid dressed up in a KKK outfit during Spirit Week and no one knocked his block off. When the Klansman was finally confronted by a faculty member, he couldn't understand what the fuss was all about. No kid in an urban school would be that insensitive.

The longer you teach, the better you get. Well, there's no myth like an old myth. This pipedream is so widely accepted that it's built into the salary schedule. Nothing else is taken into consideration. If you've taught twelve years, then you're on step twelve and get paid more than all other teachers with only, say, seven years' experience. When you hear teachers say that they have "paid their dues," it simply means that as young teachers they were overworked and underpaid. Now, when they are at the top of the salary scale, the only fair thing to do is to be underworked and overpaid.

All Asians are good in math and science. Not true. Some Asians have trouble in these subjects. And in any event, the compliment is a bit left-handed. It sounds like Asians have some genetic or dietary advantage. The fact is that most Asians are good at all subjects because they place such a high premium on academic excellence. Ever wonder why the white racists love to note the lower overall scores achieved by blacks, but never mention how much higher the average Asian scores compared to the average white kid?

Tenure is necessary in public schools to protect free speech. Tenure is not a teacher's first line of defense for free speech.

The First Amendment is. And that is particularly so since the great Supreme Court decisions of the 1960's and 1970's. Unless we start electing the likes of Catherine de Medici and Robespierre to school boards and unless all those Supreme Court decisions are reversed, I think the issue of free speech in defense of tenure is largely a red herring.

The trouble with tenure—and its next of kin, reduction in force based solely on seniority—is that it shelters the weak, the incompetent, and the burnt-out teacher at the expense of the children. So once these teachers are tenured, the school is stuck with them for the next twenty or thirty years, so long as some bare minimum standard of competence is maintained.

Grades mean something. Another popular myth. Passing grades may result from an achievement. But, more likely, they are the result of a good attendance record or an effort by the teacher to protect the kid's self-image or to avoid conflict with the parents. The best report cards require the teacher to write out their evaluation of the student, specifically spelling out strengths and weaknesses. But, as I know from personal experience, it's so much easier to write down a *B* and let it go at that. In all my years of teaching, I never had a parent call me up and ask, "Good at what? Was she good at memorizing facts? critical thinking? asking questions? participating in class?"

Dropping out of school will ruin your life. It might, but only if you let it. There are many examples of kids who finally got straightened out after coming face to face with the real world. The educational establishment *loves* to promote this myth because high enrollment protects the jobs of the membership. And, unfortunately, the public has bought this "stay in school or else" nonsense. That's why the classifieds always say, "high-school diploma required" rather than, "needed: a young person who can read and think."

High school is "the best four years of your life." The next-of-kin to "dropping out of school will ruin your life." The only people who really believe this rubbish are the ones who have been out of high school for a few years. Usually they're uncles giving unwanted advice to a nephew. Kids know that the neither-here-nor-there world between childhood and adulthood is tough on the psyche as well as the loins. What adult would seriously want to trade in his or her grown-up responsibilities and freedoms for the acne pimples, heartaches, and awkwardness of adolescence? But, if some people still insist on living in the past, I recommend a true age of innocence, say, sometime between kindergarten and the third grade.

15 *Dewey's Dictionary for Decoding Educational Jargon*

Accountability: The theory whereby the teacher takes the credit when things go right and the parent takes the blame when they don't. The teachers who have honors-level classes favor this idea.

American History: Whatever it takes to get the state of Texas to adopt your textbook.

Attendance Roll: A list of all students attending the school plus just enough ficticious students for the school to qualify for the next-highest level of state and federal aid.

Back to Basics: A movement away from classroom discussions and toward more worksheets.

Booster Club: A dedicated community organization designed to promote any and all school activities save academic.

Busing: Rich people ordering poor whites and poor blacks to move into each other's schools.

Class Rank: The official recognition that half the kids in the school are below average.

Conservative: Any teacher with tenure who asks the question, "What would I do if I were not a teacher?"

Cross-Age Tutoring: The blind leading the blind.

Curriculum Reform: The periodic revival of all courses discontinued ten years earlier.

Deschooling: The treasonous proposal to eliminate the traditional public school from the landscape.

Detention: A free, after-school baby-sitting service provided by the school. It is readily assigned by teachers who don't have to monitor the detention hall.

Differentiated Diplomas: Small, medium, and large sheepskins.

Evolution: A four-letter word to all textbook publishers.

Functional Illiterate: Someone who should be suing the school only after he sues his parents.

Gifted Child: To hear some people talk you would think that it was the average child twenty years ago.

Graduation: Regardless of what battles have been won or lost during the preceding nine months, each June the teachers declare victory and start their summer vacations. It should be renamed George Aiken Day after the late Vermont senator who once said that we should declare victory in Vietnam and go home.

Homework: At school the student will always say that there's too much; at home the student will always say that it's done.

Individualization: Letting each kid flunk at his or her own rate.

Jail Bait: An obnoxious kid in a state where there's a law against corporal punishment.

Lecture: A marvelous teaching technique designed exclusively for those students who have not yet learned to read.

Mainstreaming: I won't fish on my side. You won't fish on your side. We'll all fish in the middle.

Minimum Competence: The ability to walk and chew gum at the same time, which must be clearly demonstrated at the end of the school year. Basically, it's a public relations gesture to prove that the schools are doing something.

Multimedia Approach: Who brought the popcorn?

National Education Association: A labor organization that has been waiting since Reagan's election in 1980 for the sky to fall.

Open Classroom: A brilliant educational reform for putting all the chaos in one place. If you really want an open classroom you knock down the school, not just a few walls.

Parents: Former students who get back at the public school system by reproducing themselves.

Pedagogy: Teaching is honest labor. Beware of anyone who tries to dress it up with this pompous term.

PTA Meeting: A time for those who know very little about what children really want to get together with those who know even less.

Qualified: A term which should be substituted immediately for "certified" as an adjective in front of "teacher."

Radical: Any young teacher who wonders why he or she gets all the worst classes and receives less than half the pay of the older teachers who get all the good classes.

Reformer: Anyone who doesn't actually have to carry out the reform in the classroom.

Research Paper: A generally worthless writing exercise in which the sharp student makes just enough mistakes to convince the teacher that the paper wasn't plagiarized. Teachers who assign book reports or biographical essays are just asking for trouble.

Social Studies: American history and the seven dwarfs. The dwarfs include European history, non-western history, ancient history, geography, sociology, economics, and philosophy.

Study Hall: Where teachers compete with students to see who can best kill the hour.

Substitute Teacher: A masochist who when hired calls up the superintendent to say "thank you."

Superintendent: The only man or woman in the school district who can give a graduation speech every year with a straight face.

Tabula Rasa: The mistaken notion, first formulated by John Locke, that the score is nurture 100, nature 0. In other words, the kid was born with a blank and formless mind upon which we can write anything we want. This theory is sometimes used to nail the teacher to the wall when a kid goes sour.

Teacher Dress Code: The belief that a tie around the neck improves the circulation to the brain.

Teachers' Lounge: The black hole of education where all the teachers want to go and none of the teachers want to leave.

16 Can You Pass This Minimum-Competency Test?

General Knowledge

1. Which is most likely to be an inch long?
   A. A necktie.
   B. A baseball bat.
   C. A paper clip.
2. What is the maximum number of years a President can serve?
   A. Four years.
   B. Eight years.
   C. Ten years.
3. What is the coldest month of the year in Chile?
   A. January.
   B. February.
   C. July.
4. Imagine that you have a one-pound box. Inside the box are two pounds of bees. How much would the box and the bees weigh if all the bees were flying?
   A. One pound.
   B. Two pounds.

C. Three pounds.

5. Think of yourself standing alone in a kitchen on a hot day. You open the refrigerator door and leave it open. The temperature in the kitchen will
   A. Go up.
   B. Go down.
   C. Stay the same.

Math

6. Freddy and Clancy each have ten bananas. Freddy gives all his bananas to Clancy in exchange for a picture of Clancy's sister in her underwear. How many bananas does Freddy have?
7. If it takes three cats three days to eat three mice, how long does it take one cat to eat one mouse?
8. What are the odds of correctly predicting a three-digit state lottery number?

Geography

9. Flying due south from Mexico City, what's the first country you'll hit not counting Antarctica?
10. In air miles, which city is closer to Atlanta, Cincinnati or Miami?
11. Is Las Vegas east or west of San Diego?

U. S. History

12. Who was Vice President in 1964?
13. Who got the right to vote first, blacks or women?
14. Andrew Johnson was impeached. True or false?
15. Thomas Jefferson was one of the Founding Fathers. True or false?

Turn the page for the answers.

ANSWERS

1. C.
2. C. (The president could serve two years on someone else's term plus eight on his own.)
3. C.
4. C. (The pressure of the bees' wings on the bottom of the box weighs two pounds.)
5. A. (Unless you had a brand-new, super-efficient refrigerator the temperature would go up because of the overheating motor.)
6. None. (You're hurting if you missed this one. Go sit in the corner.)
7. 3. (If you missed this one, go join your friend who missed question 6.)
8. 999 to 1. (Not 1000 to 1.)
9. India. (If you said Canada or the Soviet Union, you can forget ever becoming a pilot.)
10. Cincinnati. (Easily.)
11. East. (But Reno is west of San Diego.)
12. No one.
13. Blacks. (When the fifteenth Amendment was ratified in 1870. Women had to wait another fifty years.)
14. True. (He was impeached, but not convicted.)
15. False. (Jefferson was in France at the time of the Constitutional Convention.)

The Ratings

13-15	correct	We're waiting for the results of the urinalysis.
10-12	correct	You must be working on your master's.
7-9	correct	Well, at least you're honest.
3-6	correct	Now aren't you glad they didn't have a minimum-competency test when you were in school?
1-2	correct	Let's see. You got the one about the paper clips and the one about Clancy's bananas.

17 *Confusion Says . . .*

After sixteen years in the classroom you're bound to learn something. Even teachers can pick up the general drift of things after a while. So I did learn something. It may not be much, but it's all I've got. What follows are some personal insights into the true nature of public education and the teaching business.

If the conversation in the faculty room is stimulating, the subject is vibrators. (That's why teachers say they need the summer vacation to get their batteries recharged.)

There really was an emergency the one time you denied a kid a bathroom pass.

Teachers sign their new contracts in the spring. Spring is also the time when unmoored girls wear fishnet sweaters. That alone was enough to get me to sign the contract for years.

If you think that the class is going well and that the kids are really learning, then you obviously know nothing about kids or teaching.

Teachers in the next town always make more money.

In poor rural towns teachers are hated because they work

only part time and get paid more than anyone else.

In rich suburban towns teachers are scoffed at because they don't make more money and because "anyone can teach."

Every school has at least one student who loves to staple the pages of your dictionary together.

The fire alarm works best when you're giving an exam.

Compulsory attendance laws are a good example of an excellent idea gone bad. We keep such laws not because they help the kids, but because they help the teachers. High attendance numbers = more teaching jobs.

Parents have all the characteristics of their children *only worse.*

The sale of indulgences continues under the name of a high-school diploma.

There's not much you can do once you have committed yourself to eating a school lunch.

Even the best teacher, sooner or later, will teach with his fly open.

If there's something you don't know about your subject, no one will discover it until you're being observed by the principal.

Teachers who can't teach are often promoted to principal on the assumption that they have to be able to do something right.

Isn't it strange that the people who think the schools are inferior are the same ones who want a longer school day and a longer school year?

Teachers who think that their summer workshop will make a big difference in the fall just haven't been paying attention. (Actually the purpose of most summer workshops is to undo the damage done by the previous summer workshop.)

Monks take a pledge of obedience, poverty, and chastity. So do young single teachers in small rural towns.

18 *What the Sages Say...*

"The founding fathers in their wisdom decided that children were an unnatural strain on parents. So they provided jails called schools, equipped with tortures called education. School is where you go between when your parents can't take you and industry can't take you." *John Updike.*

"You don't have to think too hard when you talk to a teacher." *J. D. Salinger.* (Unless, of course, you too are a teacher.)

"Why in the world are salaries higher for administrators when the basic mission is teaching?" *Governor Jerry Brown.* (Old Moonbeam was thinking clearly on this one.)

"He is either dead or teaching school." *Zenobius* in the first century B.C. (Not much of a choice.)

"Sixty years ago I knew everything; now I know nothing; education is a progressive discovery of our own ignorance." *Will Durant.* (No one knows more than a sophomore in college or a first-year teacher.)

"A teacher affects eternity; no one can tell where his influence stops." *Henry Adams.* (Half of me, at least, would still like to believe that.)

"Only great sex rivals a truly well-taught class." *Author.*

"For every person wishing to teach there are thirty not wanting to be taught." *W. C. Sellar and R. J. Yeatman.* (That, in a nutshell, is the challenge of every teacher unless, of course, the teacher is the department head and can pick and choose his or her own classes.)

"The great end of education is to discipline rather than to furnish the mind; to train it to the use of its own powers, rather than fill it with the accumulation of others." *Tryon Edwards.* (Sooner or later all teachers learn that no matter how good they are, they'll always be playing second banana to the kid's mind. Whatever students do in their lives, the final credit or blame rests with them, not their teachers.)

"The well-meaning people who talk about education as if it were a substance distributable by coupon in large or small quantities never exhibit any understanding of the truth that you cannot teach anybody anything that he does not want to learn." *George Sampson.* (You can lead a horse to water, but that doesn't mean he won't kick you in the teeth once you get there.)

"All of us learn to write in the second grade . . . most of us go on to greater things." *Bobby Knight,* college basketball coach. (On the other hand, some of us learn to scream in the second year of life and never go on to anything else.)

"The mediocre teacher tells. The good teacher explains. The superior teacher demonstrates. The great teacher inspires."

William Arthur Ward. (I've gone through all four stages in a single day. The emotional roller coaster goes with the job.)

"Soap and education are not as sudden as a massacre, but they are more deadly in the long run." *Mark Twain.* (Not to mention tenure.)

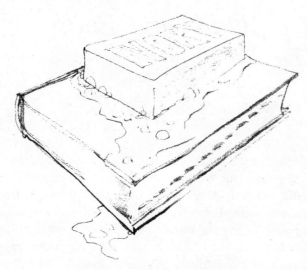

Soap and education

"Why should we subsidize intellectual curiosity?" *Ronald Reagan.* (I guess he should know.)

"My idea of education is to unsettle the minds of the young and inflame their intellects." *Robert Maynard Hutchins.* (My idea for this book is to unsettle the minds of old teachers and inflame the intellects of young teachers.)

"If there is anything education does not lack today, it is critics." *Nathan M. Pusey.* (Touché!)

19 *Odds and Ends*

Should high-school science teachers be required to teach creation science? One would have thought that this old evolution versus creation issue would have been permanently put to rest along with John T. Scopes, Clarence Darrow, and William Jennings Bryan. But not so. Every few years it rears its Adam-and-Eve head again. And one of these days the creationists might actually win a court case. If they do, what will be the consequences?

We have to assume that teachers of high-school science would be forced to present the literal interpretation of the Bible on an equal-time basis with Darwin. If I were a sincere creationist that would be the last thing on earth I would want for my children. The teacher could present my religious views in such a way as to make them look ridiculous. The tactic is an old one. Galileo wrote and published his most famous work which was, in part, entitled: *Dialogue on the Two Principal Systems of the Universe, the Ptolemaic and the Copernican, Propounding, without Deciding for Either, the Natural and Philosophical Reasons in Favor of Each.*

The speaker created by Galileo to defend the theory that the sun revolved around the earth and that the earth was the center of the solar system was named Simplicio, an apt reflection on the quality of his arguments. You would think that the creationist parent would fight to keep creationism *out* of the classroom so that it could be taught in a pure, undiluted form at home or in church. Think about it. Would you want your child to be taught American history by a Cuban Communist? Or Vermont history by a resident of New Jersey?

Should there be a law making it a federal offense for any high school senior to go directly on to college? In a word— YES! Counting nursery school and kindergarten, most high-school seniors have faced fourteen straight Septembers with a freshly scrubbed face, a pencil box, and a new pair of shoes. Enough is enough. We don't expect adults to stay at one job that long, so why should we expect it from the kids? One year of proletarian education in the fields and the factories would do any kid a world of good. Then, if the kid still wants to, he or she can go on to college.

High-school seniors have a predictable reaction to this suggestion. They hate it. On the one hand, they'll plaster the school with countdown posters proclaiming, "Only 45 days til we blow this popsicle stand" or "Just 38 days til freedom." Then in the next breath they're talking about how great it will be in college. Little do they know that it will be more of the same. Lectures they don't want to hear, research papers they don't want to write, books they don't want to read, and exams they don't want to take.

And, of course, as in high school, most of them won't have to pay for it. It is just another goose step in their preprogrammed life. Students need a year off to see if they really want to go to college. The money spent sending kids to college who really don't want to go would probably balance the national budget. And kids need a year off to discover the labor component behind the bucks that they have been spending all these years.

The most common fear that kids have about taking a year off is that they will forget everything they have learned. American students are really brainwashed when it comes to formal education. They are firmly convinced that nothing cures school like more schooling. But you can hardly blame them because they have known nothing else but school. The paper chase isn't just for Harvard law students.

Should we continue to teach our children that there's no such thing as a free lunch? Absolutely not! It may be true at Howard Johnson's, but as a maxim about life in suburbia, it's close to unadulterated flapdoodle. Sure, there is an element of truth in such a notion. Most people *do* have to work for a living. But, on a more important level, the no-free-lunch prattle reflects a disturbing and anti-historical bias. It seems that we have become a nation of professional whiners lacking any sense of human progress.

Adult attitudes are not lost on the children. As a teacher, I found students who couldn't believe that there really was a world before the Walkman and the Trans AM. With their egocentric, myopic view of reality they could scarcely accept that there was a time when an evening's entertainment consisted of a grandparent telling a tall tale around the fireplace.

The truth is, of course, that today's adults and children are pulling up a chair to the greatest free lunch of all time. We sit firmly atop the sum total of five thousand years' worth of sweat and toil. We are feasting on the political, intellectual, scientific, and artistic achievements of all past centuries. All we have to do is muster up the energy to flick on the stereo in order to savor Mozart or Gershwin or John Lennon. Or manage somehow to put one foot in front of the other to get to the museum for visual treats courtesy of Monet or Rembrandt or Picasso. No free lunch indeed!

It's more like a free banquet. We don't have to crawl out of the cave each generation to reinvent the wheel. (Although teachers insist on doing just that during most summer workshops.) We don't have to eat all the varieties of mushrooms again to see which one will drop us like a stone and which ones will cost $3 a pound. And we don't even have to wait for another genius to rediscover Preparation H. (Although I do wonder about the guy in the TV ad who says, "I always keep Preparation H *by my side*." That's not my understanding of how the product works.)

But to hear the groans from some people you would think they had had to clear the American wilderness single-handedly with a dull ax. You would think that no one had ever been more put upon. Adults act as if they were the only ones who ever had to perform a thankless task. Just as kids think they invented sex, so their parents think they invented sacrifice. Schools must once again teach the children that they have a moral obligation not just to feast but to add an entree to the next generation's free lunch. The late Will Durant said it perfectly: "Nations are born stoic and die epicurean."

Should teachers have police powers? In every study on public schools, discipline has been identified as the number one problem. Teachers are often powerless to deal with juvenile delinquents who regard a "trip to the office" as a low-level form of aerobic exercise. So the suggestion has been made that teachers be deputized. Teachers would then be able to twist arms when they weren't molding minds. In order to give the idea every chance for success, I've developed the following guidelines.

1. Issue each deputy/teacher a stun gun. It would be inconvenient to arrest a student in the middle of a lecture. With a

stun gun the teacher can just zap the miscreant without leaving the rostrum. The body could then be removed at the end of the period. Student lovers who, if they got any closer would be engaged, could also be zapped. Then the authorities could call in the parents to show them the exact nature of their children's embrace.

2. Issue each deputy/teacher a helmet with a plastic shield. This would be ideal for breaking up a food fight in the cafeteria. And, if you've ever stepped into a classroom only to be hit flush in the face with an eraser, you know another advantage to the plastic shield.

3. Issue the deputy/teacher rubber bullets and a can of mace for hall duty and potty patrol. (In some schools where the toilets are living quarters for the students who smoke cigarettes and other substances, it may be wise to carry a gas mask and a can of Lysol spray as well.) A Miranda card would seem to be essential as well.

4. If the school can afford it, how about a few well-trained police dogs? The dogs would have to be able to sit quietly during a filmstrip and not doze off or howl.

5. Hold a summer workshop to instruct the deputy/teacher to say "Assume the position" with conviction. They could also practice "Up against the locker" and "Drop those books!"

6. To look the part, the deputy/teacher would also need handcuffs, a nightstick, and one-way sunglasses.

20 *Parting Thoughts*

I gave up teaching because the bad things began to outweigh the good things and, in any event, it was just the time in my life when I needed to do something else. Still, there were some perks I'm going to miss sorely as an ex-public-school teacher. Here's a sample.

You get your name engraved on the door. Actually, if you're lucky, it may be several doors. It depends on how many bathrooms there are in the school. In the business world your name is engraved on a nameplate and screwed on to the office door. In public schools your name is carved on the inside of the toilet door. Even the best teachers can have their names linked with an anatomical impossibility on a bathroom wall.

The three-drink lunch. At six minutes a drink, most teachers can down three glasses of government-surplus milk during their lunch break. Unlike the more famous three-martini lunch, the milk cannot be deducted as a business expense even if you're talking business.

The executive dining room. Teachers call it a lounge. I call it the DMZ. Where in the business world can you find a job that has its own civil defense shelter? (Unless, of course, it's the executive washroom.) It's like a free zone in the game of Parcheesi—once you're there no one can jump you.

Free stationery. You can use all the yellow-lined paper and crayons you want to inquire about jobs in private industry. Chalk is also free, but have you ever tried to mail a blackboard?

Snow days. There is absolutely nothing as sweet as a snow day. The Boston Blizzard of 1978 was my favorite, since we had six days off in a row. But an old friend of mine recalls an even better winter. It was 1969 and one giant snowstorm cancelled the week before the February vacation and another giant storm cancelled the week after the February vacation. Those three weeks are my friend's fondest memories of public-school teaching.

snow days

Free message service. Now who would want to leave a job which has a dozen or so volunteer message-takers in the front office? Students who aspire to be secretaries have to learn some place. And, as long as the teacher doesn't insist that the message contain the name of the caller, the date, or the time, how can anyone complain? Teachers are, after all, trained to cope with ambiguity. Getting a student-volunteer message is like getting one cablegram that says simply, "Ignore earlier cable!"

No Social Security payments. This perk was especially hard to leave. With their modest salaries, teachers are not big scoopers at the public trough, but at least we Massachusetts teachers could look forward to the day when we could become double-dippers. We have our own retirement program which the taxpayers help to subsidize and our salaries are not garnished with Social Security payments. We could all, however, qualify for Social Security benefits simply by working during the summer and holding down a part-time job. That way you pay into the system maybe $200 a year rather than $2,000 a year.

Free athletic passes. As a teacher, you can see all the 28–0 JV softball games you want. And it's all free. In the business world you have to wait until it's your turn before you get tickets to see the Red Sox or the Knicks.

The summer vacation. In what other business do you get a chance to work three months of the year scooping ice cream, painting, or tending bar to make ends meet?

The kids. I'll miss the kids. Well, most of them anyway. The good kids are the biggest perk of all.